ABC

Bible
Time

Written By: Masheik

Illustrated By: Tyra Willoughby

CHAVIS
ENTERPRISES

REBIRTH PUBLISHING BOOKS FOR YOUNG READERS
A division of Chavis Enterprises Young Readers Group. Published by Chavis Enterprises (USA), Nashville, TN

Typography by Tyra Willoughby

Printed in the USA.

ISBN-13: 978-0692280799

ISBN-10:0692280790

ACKNOWLEDGEMENTS

I want to thank God who is the head of my life for allowing me to write my second childrens book. Thanks to my family and friends for being by my side every step of the way, and for supporting me in all of my dreams. Thanks to my publishing company `Chavis Enterprises' for all your help and support. God bless each and every one of you.

Enjoy!
Masheik

A is for Angels

Angels watching over me.

B is for Bible

It tells us the commandments

and the Laws of God.

C is for Cross

Jesus died on the cross
for our sins.

D is for Disciples

Jesus had 12 disciples.

E is for Eternity

When we live for Christ you will have eternal life

F is for Faith

God said all you need is faith as small

as a mustard seed.

G is for Grace

Always say grace before you eat.

H is for Halleljuah

This is the highest praise to our Father.

I is for Instrument

Praise him with music.

J is for Jewels

You are God's precious jewel.

K is for Kindness

Always have a kind heart.

L is for Laughter

Laughter is good for the soul.

M is for Mindful

Be mindful towards one another.

N is for Naughty

NO! NO! NO!

God does not want you to be naughty.

O is for Olive Tree

Living under
the olive tree.

P is for Pray

Talk to God through Prayer.

Q is for Queen

There are **60** Queens in the Bible.

R is for Rules

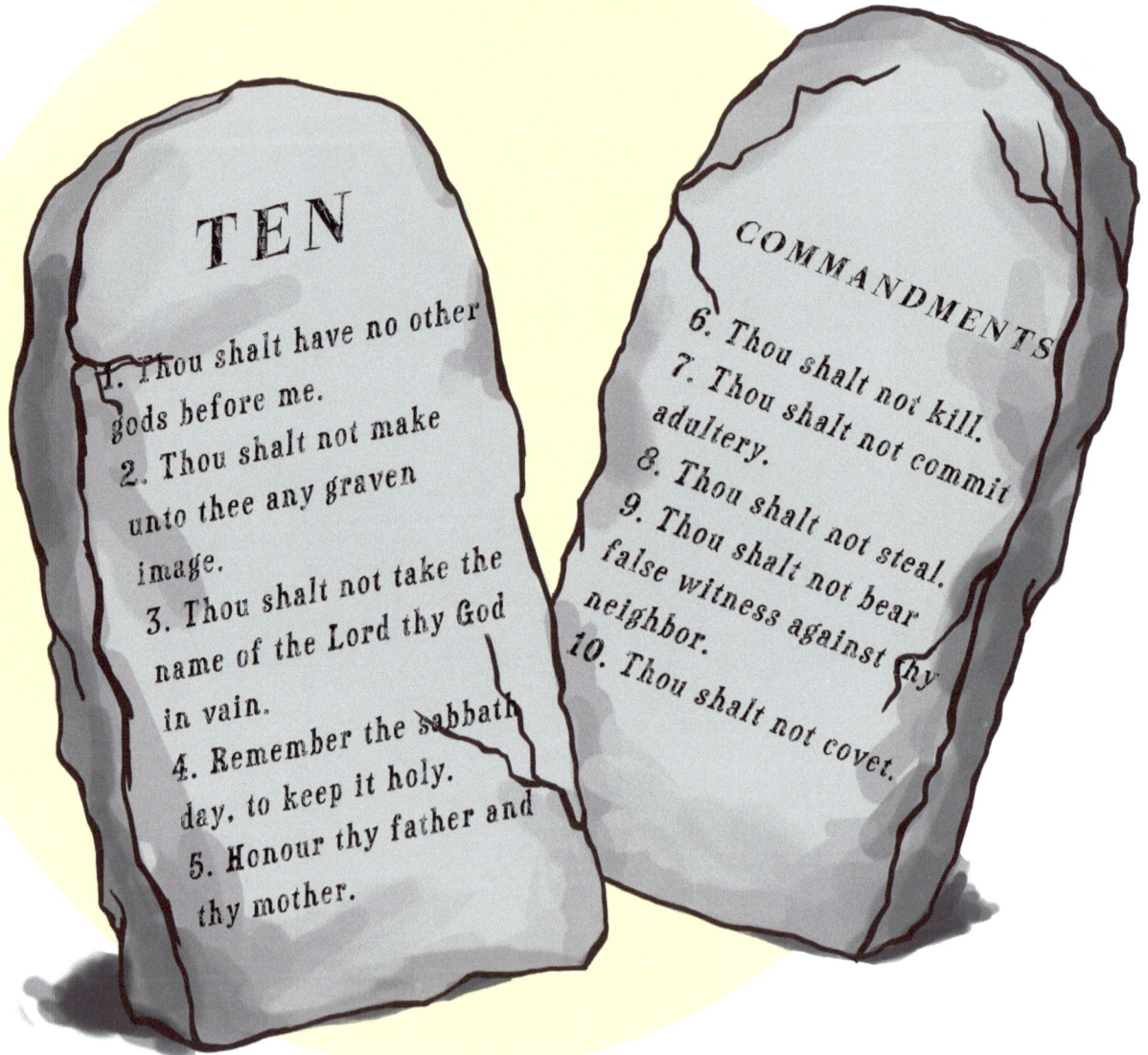

TEN

1. Thou shalt have no other gods before me.
2. Thou shalt not make unto thee any graven image.
3. Thou shalt not take the name of the Lord thy God in vain.
4. Remember the sabbath day, to keep it holy.
5. Honour thy father and thy mother.

COMMANDMENTS

6. Thou shalt not kill.
7. Thou shalt not commit adultery.
8. Thou shalt not steal.
9. Thou shalt not bear false witness against thy neighbor.
10. Thou shalt not covet.

We have to respect the rules of the Bible.

S is for Singing

Sing unto the Lord.

T is for Teacher

A pastor teaches
us life lessons.

U is for Unicorn

I can have strength like a unicorn.

V is for Victory

Victory in Jesus' name.

W is for Worship

Worshipping in the church house.

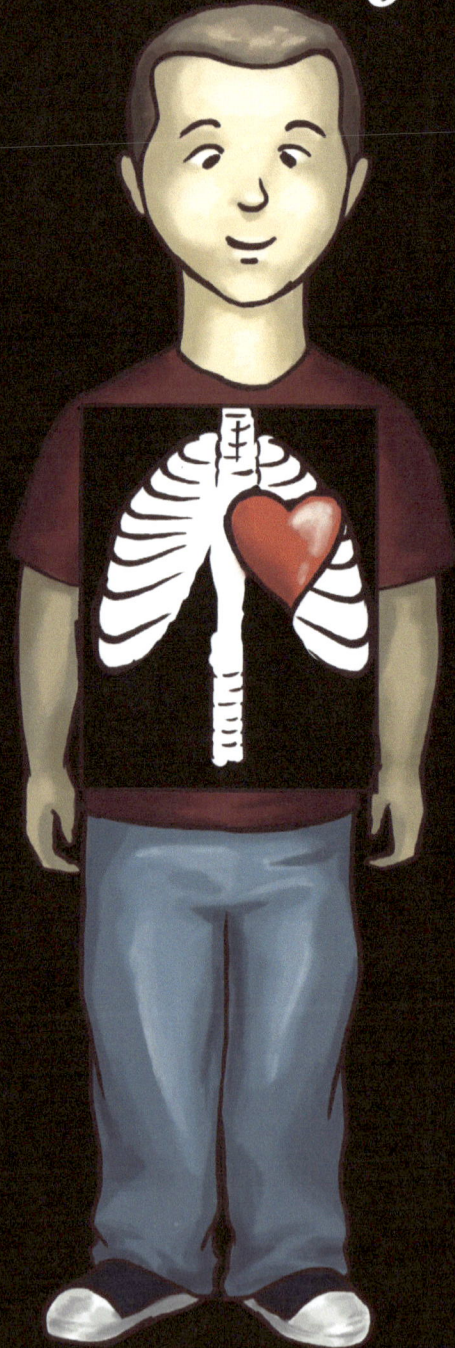

Y is for Yes

Say YES to God!

Z is for Zion

A hill on which Jerusalem was built.

www.ingramcontent.com/pod-product-compliance
Lightning Source LLC
Chambersburg PA
CBHW041550040426

42447CB00002B/122